QUICK & EASY
PASTA
SAUCES

QUICK & EASY
PASTA
SAUCES

70 imaginative recipes
for the busy cook

Shirley Gill

Howell Press

HOWELL PRESS
Published in the United States 1994 by
Howell Press, Inc., 1147 River Road,
Suite 2, Charlottesville, VA 22901.
Telephone 804–977–4006

ISBN: 0–943231–66–3

Managing Editor Samantha Gray
Art Director Jane Forster
Photographer Sue Atkinson
Home Economist Shirley Gill
Typeset by Bookworm Typesetting, Manchester
Color Separation by Scantrans Pte. Ltd., Singapore
Jacket Border by Susan Williams (Home Economist)
Edward Allwright (Photographer)
Acorn Studios plc, London
(Computer Graphics)

Printed and bound by Proost International Book Production

Contents

INTRODUCTION
6

VEGETABLE AND HERB SAUCES
10

SEAFOOD SAUCES
34

MEAT AND POULTRY SAUCES
52

CHEESE AND NUT SAUCES
69

INDEX
80

Introduction

Pasta has never been more popular – it's tasty, cheap and healthy. It is also one of the quickest and most satisfying dishes anyone can cook.

In this book, you will find both new and traditional sauces, many taking no longer to cook than the time it takes to boil a pan of water and cook the pasta! Pasta offers endless variety to the cook from sauces as simple as melted butter with freshly grated Parmesan cheese to tantalizing and extravagant sauces such as Salmon and Fennel, Confit of Duck and Mushrooms and Goat's Cheese with Prosciutto.

Many of the recipes are Italian in origin or inspiration but the flavors of other countries are also there to be explored.

For the most part the recipes in this book call upon standard ingredients that most people either have on hand or that can be bought with little difficulty in any store. There are a few specialist ingredients, such as porcini and sun-dried tomato paste, which are worth hunting for in Italian delicatessens.

Lastly, good-quality ingredients are essential to the very basics of pasta sauce-making. Tomato is indispensable for flavor and color in many recipes. Use firm, ripe plum tomatoes whenever possible; canned plum tomatoes are an excellent substitute. Use fresh herbs, especially basil and parsley, and a good olive oil – extra-virgin is the best grade.

EQUIPMENT

There are a few basic utensils which you should try to have on hand. A large, good-quality saucepan is essential; every 1 pound of pasta needs to be cooked in at least 7 pints of water so that it can move freely without touching and sticking together. For draining, a colander is needed, preferably one with legs that will stand up by itself in the sink. Alternatively, you can use a proper pasta pan, which has an inner basket so that the pasta may be lifted from the water with ease. Other essential items are a long-handled spoon or fork for stirring the pasta while cooking, as well as a special fork for removing spaghetti and a grater for grating Parmesan cheese.

Another useful implement is a Parmesan knife, designed not to cut but to allow you to put pressure on a certain point so that the desired piece is broken off.

PASTA VARIETIES
The word 'pasta' means paste or dough in Italian. It is made from a special grain called durum wheat, which produces semolina when ground. The majority of pasta is made from semolina flour mixed with water. Pasta *all'uovo* is made with eggs, and both types are interchangeable. They are available dried and sold in packages. Commercial fresh pasta is widely available. There are two main types: flat or shaped and stuffed. Pasta made with whole-wheat flour is also available. Whole-wheat pasta has a rich brown color and contains much more fiber; it also takes longer to cook.

Pasta dough can be left plain or flavored and colored with additions such as tomato paste, chopped herbs or spinach, crushed garlic or beet juice. Black pasta is produced by coloring the pasta dough with the ink from squid or octopus.

COOKING PASTA
Always cook pasta in plenty of boiling salted water. A tablespoon of oil added to the water will help prevent the pasta sticking and the water from boiling over. When the water comes to a rolling boil, add the

pasta, stirring from time to time as it cooks. Dried long pasta such as spaghetti must be bent slowly into the water as it softens, and shake loose coils of fresh pasta before cooking.

Follow cooking directions on the package for dried pasta. Fresh pasta cooks more quickly than dried, usually in 3-5 minutes or when it rises to the surface. Test frequently to make sure it does not overcook. It should still be firm to the bite – *al dente*.

Once cooked, pour a cupful of cold water into the pan to stop further cooking. Drain immediately in a colander and shake carefully – a little water should still cling to it. Return to the saucepan or transfer to a hot serving dish and add a tablespoon of butter or oil; toss well and serve immediately.

SERVING PASTA

The Italians have very definite views about which sauce should be served with which pasta. The texture, thickness and shape of the pasta play an important role in this pairing. For example, long thin strands such as spaghetti and linguine are best with light olive oil, strongly flavored tomato-, seafood- and egg-based sauces. Pasta shells, twists, thick tubes and quills need thick sauces that become trapped in their folds, curls and hollows. Thick strips such as tagliatelle and pappardelle go well with cheese and meat-based sauces. Stuffed pastas call for subtle sauces.

THE HEALTHY OPTION

Pasta is a good source of protein, fiber and energy and, contrary to popular belief, is not fattening if served with a low-calorie sauce. There are also plenty of alternatives to ingredients with a high-fat content. For example, you can often replace cream with yogurt, substitute skim or low fat (2%) for whole fat milk and use reduced-fat and low-fat cheeses instead of full-fat types.

8

Watch out, too, for the amount of Parmesan cheese you use – 1 tablespoon contains about 70 calories.

PASTA PORTIONS
As a general guide when cooking pasta, allow 3-4 oz of dried pasta per person for a main course and 2 oz for a first course, varying the quantity according to the richness of the sauce. You will need double the quantity if using fresh pasta.

PARMESAN CHEESE: THE ESSENTIAL EXTRA
If cheese is added to a pasta dish use a good-quality, aged variety such as Parmesan (the best will be marked Parmigiano-Reggiano on the rind). Always buy fresh Parmesan, not the drums of ready-grated cheese as there is no comparison in flavor.

STORING PASTA
Dried pasta is an excellent standby to have in your pantry. It will keep almost indefinitely if you store it in a dry, dark place. Dried pasta made with eggs does not keep as well. Fresh pasta will keep for up to 48 hours in the refrigerator. The length of time stuffed fresh pasta can be kept in the refrigerator depends on the type of filling. Fresh pasta can be frozen for up to two months.

Marinated Tomato and Herb

INGREDIENTS

Serves 4

1½ pounds firm, ripe tomatoes (preferably plum)

2 garlic cloves, minced

2 tbsp shredded fresh basil

2 tbsp chopped fresh parsley

scant ½ cup olive oil

salt and black pepper

1   Plunge the tomatoes into a bowl of hot water and leave for 1 minute. Drain and refresh under cold water. Peel, deseed and chop the flesh into small cubes.

2   Place the chopped tomatoes in a bowl with the garlic, basil, parsley and oil. Season generously and mix thoroughly.

3   Leave in a cool place for about 1 hour to allow the flavors to infuse.

4   Spoon over freshly cooked pasta and serve at once.

Roasted Fennel with Lemon

1 Trim the fennel, reserving the feathery tops to garnish. Brush all over with oil and roast in the oven at 350°F for about 40 minutes. Cool slightly and chop.

2 Meanwhile beat together the butter, herbs, lemon zest and juice. Add seasoning to taste.

3 Toss the fennel and lemon and basil butter into freshly cooked pasta. Sprinkle with the Parmesan cheese and garnish with the reserved fennel tops. Serve at once.

INGREDIENTS

Serves 4

2 large bulbs of Florence fennel

olive oil for brushing

½ cup sweet butter

3 tbsp fresh mixed basil and parsley, chopped

2 tsp finely grated lemon zest

1 tbsp lemon juice

salt and black pepper

½ cup freshly grated Parmesan cheese

Pepper and Mozzarella

INGREDIENTS

Serves 4

2 yellow or red bell
peppers

2 tbsp olive oil

1 onion, chopped

2 garlic cloves, minced

1 eggplant, cubed

1½ pounds ripe tomatoes,
peeled, deseeded and
chopped

1 tbsp tomato paste

salt and black pepper

¼ pound Mozzarella

1 tbsp chopped parsley

1 tbsp chopped fresh
oregano

1 Place the peppers under a hot broiler for about 10 minutes, turning occasionally, until the skins are evenly blistered and charred. Leave to cool for a few minutes then peel away and discard the skins. Cut the peppers in half, discard the seeds and roughly chop the flesh.

2 Heat the oil in a large pan and fry the onion until soft. Add the garlic and eggplant and cook for 2 minutes.

3 Add the roasted peppers, tomatoes, tomato paste and seasoning. Cover and cook for 15 minutes, stirring occasionally.

4 Toss the sauce into freshly cooked pasta with cubed Mozzarella and herbs. Serve at once.

COOK'S TIP
Add the Mozzarella cheese at the last minute so the pieces melt deliciously into the hot pasta.

Roasted Garlic and Herb

1   Break up the head of garlic, leaving each clove in its papery skin.

2   Heat 4 tbsp of the oil in a small roasting tin at 375°F, add the garlic and roast for 10-15 minutes until tender and golden brown.

3   Using a slotted spoon, transfer the garlic to a plate and remove the papery skins.

4   Roughly chop the herbs in a food processor. With the machine running slowly, pour in the remaining oil and blend to a thick paste. Stir in the roasted garlic and season to taste.

5   Toss the sauce with freshly cooked pasta and serve with Parmesan cheese.

INGREDIENTS

Serves 4

1 large head of garlic

scant cup olive oil

1 cup fresh mixed herbs
(basil, parsley, thyme and marjoram)

salt and black pepper

freshly grated Parmesan cheese

Spring Vegetable

INGREDIENTS

Serves 4

1 cup sliced, small leeks

6 oz baby carrots

1½ cups asparagus, cut
into 2-inch pieces

1 cup frozen petits pois

2 tbsp olive oil

¼ cup butter

2 shallots, chopped

3 tbsp chopped fresh
mixed herbs, such as
parsley, thyme and sage

1 cup whipping cream

¼ cup grated Parmesan
cheese

1   Cook the vegetables separately in boiling salted water making sure they remain crisp. Drain thoroughly.

2   Heat the oil and butter in a large skillet. Add the shallots and cook until softened.

3   Stir in the herbs and cream and cook gently until the sauce thickens slightly.

4   Remove the pan from the heat and stir in the Parmesan cheese. Season with salt and pepper.

5   Carefully toss the vegetables into freshly cooked pasta, then spoon the sauce over. Serve at once.

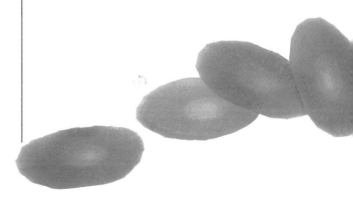

Sicilian Cauliflower

1 Break the cauliflower into flowerets, then cook in boiling salted water for 4-5 minutes until just tender. Drain well, reserving the cooking liquid.

2 Meanwhile, put the saffron strands in a small bowl with 2 tbsp hot water and leave to soak.

3 Heat the oil in a large skillet, add the onion and cook until softened. Stir in the anchovies and crush with the back of a wooden spoon until they have dissolved.

4 Stir in the saffron liquid, pine nuts, raisins and cauliflower with about 6 tbsp of the reserved cooking liquid. Cook for a further 2-3 minutes.

5 Gently toss the sauce into freshly cooked pasta. Scatter the basil on top and serve at once. Hand the cheese around separately.

INGREDIENTS

Serves 4

1 cauliflower

salt and black pepper

a good pinch of saffron strands

¼ cup olive oil

1 onion, chopped

4 anchovy fillets, drained and chopped

½ cup pine nuts, toasted

⅓ cup seedless raisins

shredded basil leaves

grated pecorino or Parmesan cheese

Sun-dried Tomato and Shallot

INGREDIENTS

Serves 4

2 tbsp butter

2 tbsp oil from a jar of
sun-dried tomatoes

1 1/2 cups thinly sliced
shallots

3 oz sun-dried tomatoes
in oil (drained weight),
chopped

1 garlic clove, minced

6 tbsp fresh parsley,
chopped

black pepper

6 oz feta cheese in oil
with herbs (drained
weight)

1   Heat the butter and oil in a skillet. Add the shallots and cook gently, stirring occasionally until golden brown.

2   Add the sun-dried tomatoes, garlic and parsley. Cook, stirring, for 1-2 minutes until hot. Stir in the feta cheese. Season to taste with pepper.

3   Spoon the sauce onto freshly cooked pasta and serve at once.

16

Asparagus with Prosciutto

1 Trim the aspara-
gus and cut into 3-inch
pieces. Cook in boiling salted
water for 6-8 minutes or until just
tender.

2 Meanwhile, place the cream, Gruyère and Parmesan cheeses in
a small saucepan and heat gently, stirring constantly until just
boiling. Remove from the heat and season lightly with salt and
pepper.

3 Drain the asparagus and toss into freshly cooked pasta with the
prosciutto. Spoon the sauce over and sprinkle with a little nutmeg.
Serve at once, sprinkled with Parmesan cheese.

COOK'S TIP
Thinly sliced, cooked ham can be substituted for the prosciutto.

INGREDIENTS

Serves 4

¾ pound asparagus

scant 1 cup light cream

¼ cup grated Gruyère
cheese

¼ cup freshly grated
Parmesan cheese

salt and white pepper

2 oz prosciutto, cut into
strips

freshly grated nutmeg

freshly grated Parmesan
cheese (optional)

Leek and Pancetta

INGREDIENTS

Serves 4

1 cup halved snap beans

salt and black pepper

1 ½ cups sliced small leeks

¼ cup butter

¼ pound pancetta or smoked bacon, cut into strips

1 garlic clove, minced

½ cup full-fat cream cheese with garlic and herbs

6 tbsp light cream

grated Parmesan cheese (optional)

1   Cook the snap beans in boiling salted water for about 6 minutes until almost tender. Add the leeks and simmer for a further 2 minutes. Drain well.

2   Melt the butter in a saucepan, add the pancetta or bacon and garlic and fry for 3 minutes. Add the beans and leeks and cook for a further minute.

3   Meanwhile, blend together the soft cheese and cream. Warm through gently, stirring continuously. Season with pepper to taste.

4   Add the leek and pancetta mixture to freshly cooked pasta. Spoon the sauce over and serve at once, dusted with Parmesan cheese if liked.

COOK'S TIP
Look out for pancetta in Italian delicatessens. Similar to bacon, but with a very distinct flavor of its own, it is excellent for adding to stews, sauces and vegetable dishes.

Borlotti Bean and Mushroom

1 Heat the oil in a skillet and fry the shallots until soft. Add the garlic and mushrooms and fry for about 2 minutes.

2 Add the oregano and borlotti beans and heat through gently. Taste and adjust the seasoning.

3 Toss the sauce with freshly cooked pasta. Sprinkle generously with chives and serve with Parmesan cheese sprinkled on top.

INGREDIENTS

Serves 4

6 tbsp olive oil

2 shallots, chopped

2-3 garlic cloves, minced

2½ cups sliced mixed fresh mushrooms

1 tbsp chopped fresh oregano

15 oz can borlotti beans, rinsed and drained

salt and black pepper

snipped fresh chives

freshly grated Parmesan cheese to garnish

Peppers with Saffron and Basil

INGREDIENTS

Serves 4

2 large red bell
peppers

2 large yellow bell
peppers

a good pinch of saffron
strands

2 tbsp olive oil

1 garlic clove, minced

1 red onion, chopped

12-15 fresh basil leaves,
roughly torn

²/₃ cup whipping cream

salt and black pepper

grated Parmesan cheese

basil leaves to garnish

1   Place the peppers under a hot broiler for about 10 minutes, turning occasionally, until the skins are evenly blistered and charred (the skins are not eaten).

2   Meanwhile, put the saffron strands in a bowl with 2 tbsp hot water and leave to soak.

3   Leave the peppers to cool for a few minutes, then peel away and discard the skins. Cut the peppers in half, discard the seeds and cut the flesh into cubes.

4   Heat the oil in a skillet, add the garlic and onion and cook until softened. Add the peppers, saffron liquid, basil and cream. Cook for a few minutes until heated through. Do not allow the peppers to become mushy.

5   Taste and adjust the seasoning then toss the sauce into freshly cooked pasta. Sprinkle with Parmesan cheese and serve at once, garnished with basil leaves.

Garlic and Oil

1 Heat the oil in a saucepan and add the garlic. Very gently fry the garlic until it begins to color but does not brown, stirring occasionally.

2 Add the freshly cooked pasta and parsley and toss to coat each strand in the flavored oil.

3 Grind some black pepper over and serve at once.

COOK'S TIP
For extra flavor, add 1-2 deseeded finely chopped red chilies to the heated oil with the garlic.

INGREDIENTS

Serves 4 as an appetizer

½ cup olive oil

2-3 garlic cloves, minced

2 tbsp chopped fresh parsley

black pepper

Pesto

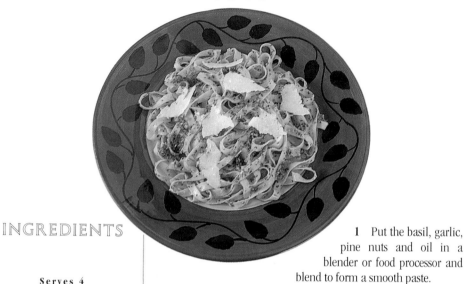

INGREDIENTS

Serves 4

large bunch of basil
leaves, about 1 cup, stems
removed

2 garlic cloves, minced

⅓ cup pine nuts

½ cup olive oil

2 tbsp butter, softened

½ cup freshly grated
Parmesan cheese

salt and black pepper

shavings of Parmesan
cheese

1   Put the basil, garlic,
pine nuts and oil in a
blender or food processor and
blend to form a smooth paste.

2   Transfer to a bowl and stir in the butter and cheese. Taste and
adjust the seasoning.

3   Toss the sauce with freshly cooked pasta and serve immediately with extra Parmesan cheese sprinkled on top.

COOK'S TIP
To store pesto, spoon into a jar and cover with a thin layer of olive
oil. Cover tightly and keep in the refrigerator for up to 1 week. Use
also for salad dressings, savory butters and vegetable soups.

Chili-Tomato with Olives

1 Heat the oil in a saucepan and fry the garlic and chili for a few minutes without browning.

2 Add the anchovies, mashing them with a fork, then add the tomatoes, sun-dried tomatoes, capers, olives and seasoning.

3 Cook gently, uncovered, for about 10 minutes, stirring occasionally. Taste and adjust seasoning if necessary.

4 Toss the sauce with freshly cooked pasta and sprinkle generously with chopped parsley. Serve at once.

COOK'S TIP
If fresh tomatoes are pale and lacking in flavor, use two 14½ oz cans of chopped tomatoes.

INGREDIENTS

Serves 4

3 tbsp oil from a jar of sun-dried tomatoes

2 garlic cloves, minced

1-2 fresh red chilies, deseeded and chopped

6 anchovy fillets, drained

1½ pounds ripe tomatoes, peeled, deseeded and chopped

¼ cup sun-dried tomatoes in oil, drained and chopped

2 tbsp rinsed and drained capers

16 ripe olives

Salt and pepper

Golden Onion with Rosemary

INGREDIENTS

Serves 4

¼ cup butter

2 tbsp olive oil

1½ pounds onions, thinly
sliced

1 tbsp fresh rosemary,
chopped

a pinch of sugar

salt and black pepper

6 tbsp dry white wine

¼ cup whipping cream

2 tbsp chopped fresh
parsley

½ cup freshly grated
Parmesan cheese

1 Heat the butter and oil in a heavy-based saucepan or flameproof casserole. Add the onions, rosemary, sugar, salt and black pepper. Cover and cook for 15-20 minutes, stirring occasionally. Taste and adjust seasoning if necessary.

2 Uncover and continue cooking, stirring occasionally, until the onions are golden brown.

3 Pour in the wine and cook over a high heat until it has evaporated. Stir in the cream and parsley and heat through gently. Taste and adjust the seasoning if necessary.

4 Spoon the sauce over freshly cooked pasta and serve with the Parmesan cheese sprinkled on top.

COOK'S TIP
If rosemary isn't your favorite herb, use sage instead.

Tomato and Basil

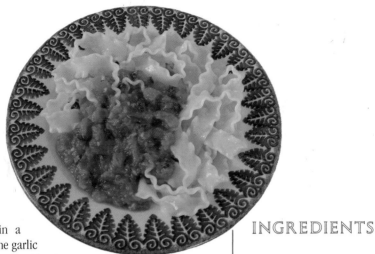

1 Heat the oil in a saucepan and fry the garlic for a few minutes without browning.

2 Stir in the tomatoes, sun-dried tomato paste, sugar, salt and pepper. Cover and cook for 15-20 minutes, stirring occasionally.

3 Add the shredded basil leaves to the sauce just before tossing with freshly cooked pasta.

COOK'S TIP
Look out for sun-dried tomato paste in delicatessens. It has a richer flavor than ordinary tomato paste. If you can't find it, tip a jar of sun-dried tomatoes in oil into a food processor and process until finely chopped. Return the paste to the jar and store in the refrigerator until needed.

INGREDIENTS

Serves 4

$\frac{1}{4}$ cup olive oil

3 garlic cloves, minced

$1\frac{1}{2}$ pounds ripe tomatoes (preferably plum), peeled, deseeded and chopped

2 tbsp sun-dried tomato paste

a pinch of sugar

salt and black pepper

10-12 fresh basil leaves, shredded

Tapenade

INGREDIENTS

Serves 4-6

1 cup pitted ripe olives in
brine, drained

2 tbsp rinsed and drained
capers

8 anchovy fillets, drained

2 garlic cloves, minced

¼ tsp dried marjoram

6 tbsp olive oil

black pepper

fresh herb sprigs
to garnish

1 Put the olives, capers, anchovies, garlic and marjoram in a blender or food processor.

2 With the machine running, gradually add the oil to form a smooth paste. Season to taste with pepper. Serve with freshly cooked pasta, garnished with herb sprigs.

COOK'S TIP
Spoon any leftover tapenade into a clean jar. Pour a thin layer of olive oil over and seal tightly. Keep in the refrigerator for up to 1 week. It is also delicious served on fresh or toasted bread, with sliced hard-cooked eggs or with a platter of crudités, including carrots, cauliflower flowerets, sticks of celery and peppers.

Tofu with Cashew Nut

1 Mix together the soy sauce, sherry, sugar, ginger, garlic and five-spice powder. Add the tofu, toss well and leave to marinate for 20 minutes. Drain, reserving the marinade.

2 Heat the oil in a skillet, add the cashew nuts and cook for 2-3 minutes until lightly browned. Remove and set aside.

3 Add the tofu and stir-fry until lightly browned. Add the green onions, cut into strips, bean sprouts and spinach, stir-fry for 1 minute over a high heat.

4 Pour in the reserved marinade and heat through. Toss with freshly cooked pasta, sprinkle with the cashew nuts and serve.

INGREDIENTS

Serves 3-4

3 tbsp dark soy sauce

2 tbsp medium-dry sherry

2 tsp soft brown sugar

1 tbsp grated fresh ginger

1 garlic clove, minced

1/2 tsp five-spice powder

1/2 pound tofu, cubed

3 tbsp peanut oil

1/2 cup salted cashew nuts

6 green onions

1 1/4 cups mixed bean sprouts

1 cup shredded young spinach leaves

Mixed Mushroom

INGREDIENTS

Serves 4

1 tbsp dried porcini
mushrooms

1 small onion, finely
chopped

¼ cup butter

1 garlic clove, minced

3 cups sliced button
mushrooms

⅔ cup whipping cream

salt and black pepper

2 tbsp chopped fresh flat-
leaved parsley

freshly grated Parmesan
cheese (optional)

1 Soak the dried porcini in just enough warm water to cover for about 20 minutes. Remove with a slotted spoon and slice. Reserve the soaking liquid for step 3.

2 In a skillet, fry the onion in the butter until softened. Add the garlic and fry for a few minutes more. Add the dried porcini and sliced button mushrooms and sauté for 3-4 minutes.

3 Add the reserved soaking liquid and cream and allow to bubble over a high heat for a few minutes until reduced by half. Season with salt and pepper.

4 Toss the sauce into freshly cooked pasta with the parsley. Serve immediately with Parmesan cheese, if liked.

COOK'S TIP
You will find dried porcini mushrooms in Italian delicatessens and some major supermarkets. Just a small amount will improve the flavor of a dish. About 1 tbsp is the equivalent of 2 cups of fresh mushrooms.

Shredded Zucchini

1 Heat the oil in a wok or large skillet. When hot, add the zucchini and garlic. Stir-fry for 2-3 minutes until the zucchini shreds start to turn color.

2 Remove from the heat and add the herbs, salt and plenty of pepper (preferably freshly ground).

3 Toss with freshly cooked pasta and serve with the Parmesan cheese sprinkled on top.

INGREDIENTS

Serves 4

3 tbsp olive oil

1 pound zucchini, trimmed and coarsely grated

2 garlic cloves, minced

3 tbsp chopped fresh mixed herbs, such as basil and parsley

salt and black pepper

1/2 cup freshly grated Parmesan cheese

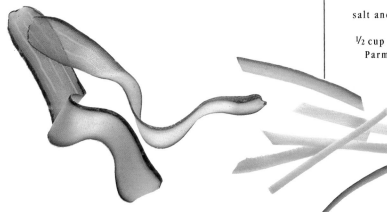

Creamy Broccoli

INGREDIENTS

Serves 4

2 tbsp olive oil

1/4 pound bacon, cut into strips

2 garlic cloves, minced

2 cups small broccoli flowerets

1/4 cup dry vermouth

1/2 cup cream cheese

2/3 cup light cream

2 tbsp chopped fresh mixed herbs, such as parsley, thyme and oregano

black pepper

shavings of Parmesan cheese

1   Heat the oil in a heavy-based saucepan. Fry the bacon until it just begins to brown.

2   Add the garlic and fry for a further minute, then add the broccoli and stir thoroughly.

3   Pour in the vermouth and cover with a tight-fitting lid. Cook for about 3 minutes, shaking the pan occasionally until the broccoli is tender but still retains some bite.

4   Add the cheese, cream and herbs and cook, stirring, until the cheese melts and forms a smooth sauce. Season with pepper.

5   Toss the sauce with freshly cooked pasta and serve at once with shavings of Parmesan cheese sprinkled on top.

Chick-pea with Coriander

1 Reserve a few whole chick-peas for the garnish. Place the remainder in a blender or food processor with the cumin, garlic, lemon juice and oil. Process until the mixture forms a paste.

2 Transfer the mixture to a bowl and stir in the yogurt and coriander. Season to taste with salt and pepper.

3 Spoon the sauce onto hot pasta and serve at once, garnished with the whole chick-peas and coriander sprigs.

INGREDIENTS

Serves 4

14 oz can chick-peas, rinsed and drained

2 tsp ground cumin

2 garlic cloves, roughly chopped

2 tbsp lemon juice or to taste

6 tbsp olive oil

2 tbsp plain yogurt

2 tbsp chopped fresh coriander

salt and black pepper

coriander sprigs to garnish

31

Spicy Avocado

INGREDIENTS

Serves 4 as an appetizer

2 ripe avocados

1 tbsp lemon juice

1 large tomato, peeled,
deseeded and chopped

3 green onions minced

1 green chili, deseeded
and chopped

2 tbsp chopped fresh
coriander

3 tbsp olive oil

salt and black pepper

sour cream (optional)

coriander sprigs to
garnish

1 Cut the avocados in half lengthwise and remove the seeds. Peel and chop the flesh into a bowl. Sprinkle the lemon juice over and mash with a fork to form a pulp.

2 Stir in the tomato, green onions, chili, coriander and oil. Season to taste with salt and pepper.

3 Spoon onto freshly cooked pasta and serve with sour cream, if liked. Garnish with coriander sprigs.

Pea and Ham

1   Heat the oil and fry the onion until it just begins to color.

2   Add the peas and cook over a low heat for 5-8 minutes, adding the bouillon gradually to prevent them drying out.

3   Add the ham, half the Parmesan cheese and pepper to taste.

4   Toss with freshly cooked pasta and serve sprinkled with the remaining Parmesan cheese.

COOK'S TIP
The amount of bouillon used in this recipe is quite small, so watch carefully that it does not evaporate completely during cooking. If necessary, add a little extra.

INGREDIENTS

Serves 3-4

3 tbsp olive oil

1 onion, chopped

1 1/2 cups frozen petits pois, thawed

6 tbsp vegetable bouillon

1 1/4 cups cubed lean cooked ham

1/3 cup freshly grated Parmesan cheese

black pepper

33

Pink Shrimp

INGREDIENTS

Serves 4 as an appetizer

3 tbsp olive oil

2 garlic cloves, minced

1 tbsp tomato paste

6 tbsp dry white wine

1 cup shelled cooked shrimp

1¼ cups light cream

salt and white pepper

2 tbsp fresh parsley, chopped

flat-leaved parsley sprigs

1   Heat the oil in a saucepan and fry the garlic for a few seconds. Stir in the tomato paste and wine and cook for a further 2-3 minutes over a low heat, stirring occasionally.

2   Add the shrimp and cook, stirring, for 2 minutes. Transfer the shrimp mixture to a blender or food processor and process until the mixture is completely smooth.

3   Return the shrimp mixture to the saucepan with the cream and reheat very gently. Season with salt and pepper. Stir in the chopped parsley.

4   Toss the sauce with freshly cooked pasta and serve at once, garnished with flat-leaved parsley sprigs.

Smoked Trout with Avocado

1 Cut the avocado in half and remove the seed. Peel and slice the flesh into a bowl. Sprinkle the lemon juice over to prevent the avocado slices becoming discolored.

2 Heat the crème fraîche or sour cream and cream in a small saucepan until slightly thickened. Remove the pan from the heat and gently stir in the trout, avocado and lumpfish roe.

3 Toss the sauce carefully into hot pasta and serve at once, garnished with chives.

INGREDIENTS

Serves 4

1 avocado

1 tbsp lemon juice

2/3 cup crème fraîche or sour cream

2/3 cup whipping cream

1/2 pound smoked trout fillets, flaked

1 tbsp red lumpfish roe

fresh chives to garnish

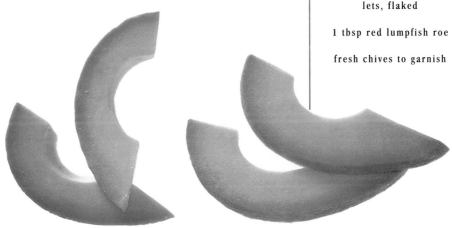

Chili-Shrimp with Snow Peas

INGREDIENTS

Serves 4

½ cup olive oil

6 oz snow peas

2 garlic cloves, minced

2 red chilies, deseeded
and chopped

¾ pound large shelled
cooked shrimp

1-2 tsp soy sauce

black pepper

2 tbsp sesame seeds,
toasted

1   Heat the oil in a skillet, add the snow peas and stir-fry for 2 minutes, stirring regularly with the heat on high.

2   Add the garlic, chilies and shrimp and fry for a further 2 minutes. Season to taste with soy sauce and pepper.

3   Toss into freshly cooked pasta and sprinkle over the toasted sesame seeds. Serve at once.

Red Clam

1 Scrub the clams and put in a large saucepan with the wine. Cook, covered, over a high heat for 3-5 minutes until the shells open. Discard any that remain closed. Strain, reserving the cooking liquid. Remove and discard the shells of half the clams.

2 Heat the oil and fry the garlic for 2 minutes. Stir in the tomatoes, sun-dried tomato paste and reserved cooking liquid. Cook gently for about 15 minutes, stirring occasionally, until the sauce thickens.

3 Add the clams and parsley and heat through gently. Season with salt and freshly ground black pepper.

4 Toss the clam sauce into freshly cooked pasta and serve.

COOK'S TIP
If fresh clams are unavailable use jars or cans of clams. Omit the wine and use 6 tbsp of clam liquid instead.

INGREDIENTS

Serves 4

2 pounds fresh baby clams

½ cup dry white wine

¼ cup olive oil

2 garlic cloves, minced

1 pound ripe tomatoes, peeled, deseeded and chopped

1 tbsp sun-dried tomato paste

2 tbsp fresh parsley, chopped

salt and black pepper

Crab with Chive

INGREDIENTS

Serves 4 as an appetizer

6 tbsp butter

2 green onions, white part only, chopped

½ pound white crab meat

a large pinch of ground mace

a large pinch of ground ginger

6 tbsp whipping cream

salt and black pepper

2 tbsp snipped fresh chives

1 Melt the butter in a saucepan, add the green onions and fry for 1 minute.

2 Stir in the crab meat, mace, ginger and cream. Cook over a low heat, stirring, until warmed through. Season to taste.

3 Spoon the crab sauce onto freshly cooked pasta. Sprinkle with chives and serve at once.

COOK'S TIP
Use either fresh or frozen and thawed crab meat for this recipe. Check the crab meat very carefully to make sure it does not contain any loose pieces of shell.

Smoked Salmon and Dill

1   Heat the butter and crème fraîche or sour cream in a small saucepan until the butter melts.

2   Add the smoked salmon, dill and seasoning. Cook for a further 1-2 minutes until heated through.

3   Toss the sauce with freshly cooked pasta. Serve at once with a little extra pepper ground over the top. Garnish with dill sprigs.

COOK'S TIP
To cut the smoked salmon into strips, roll up each slice tightly, then cut across and shake the strips to separate them.

INGREDIENTS

Serves 4 as an appetizer

2 tbsp butter

1¼ cups crème fraîche or
sour cream

½ pound smoked salmon,
cut into strips

1 tbsp chopped fresh dill

salt and black pepper

dill sprigs to garnish

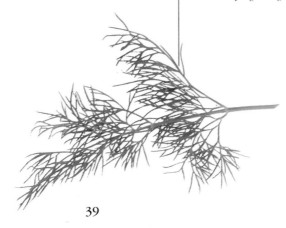

Saffron-Mussel

INGREDIENTS

Serves 4

4 pounds live mussels

²/₃ cup dry white wine

2 shallots, chopped

2 tbsp butter

2 garlic cloves, minced

1 cup whipping cream

a generous pinch of
saffron strands

1 egg yolk

salt and black pepper

1   Scrub the mussels under cold running water. Remove the beards and discard any mussels that are open.

2   Place the mussels in a large saucepan with the wine and shallots. Cover and cook over a high heat, shaking the pan frequently, for 5-8 minutes or until the mussels have opened. Drain the mussels, reserving the liquid. Discard any that remain closed. Shell the mussels, reserving a few for the garnish, and keep warm.

3   Bring the reserved cooking liquid to a boil, then reduce by half. Melt the butter in a separate pan and fry the garlic for 1 minute. Pour in the mussel liquid, cream and saffron strands. Heat gently until the sauce thickens slightly. Remove from the heat and stir in the egg yolk, mussels and seasoning to taste.

4   Spoon onto freshly cooked pasta. Garnish with the reserved mussels and serve at once.

COOK'S TIP
Adding the saffron strands just before serving, instead of soaking them in the usual way, allows the rich aroma to be appreciated.

Mediterranean Squid

1 Cut the body of the squid across into rings and leave the clusters of tentacles whole.

2 Heat the oil in a saucepan and fry the onions until just beginning to color. Add the squid and garlic and fry for a few minutes until the squid becomes firm and pink.

3 Pour in the wine and boil for about 2 minutes before adding the tomatoes, tomato paste, bay leaf, oregano and seasoning. Cover and simmer for about 30 minutes, stirring occasionally, until the squid is tender and the sauce has thickened. Remove and discard the bay leaf.

4 Toss the sauce into freshly cooked pasta with the chopped parsley. Serve at once.

COOK'S TIP
Look out for cleaned squid in major supermarkets or ask your fishmonger in advance to prepare it for you.

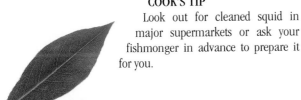

INGREDIENTS

Serves 4

1½ pounds cleaned small or medium squid

¼ cup olive oil

2 onions, chopped

2 garlic cloves, minced

½ cup red wine

1 pound ripe tomatoes, peeled, deseeded and chopped

2 tbsp tomato paste

1 bay leaf

2 tsp fresh oregano, chopped

salt and black pepper

2 tbsp fresh parsley

Shrimp in Curried Cream

INGREDIENTS

Serves 4

2 tbsp butter

1 shallot, chopped

1 tbsp mild curry powder

½ cup dry white wine

1¼ cups whipping cream

¾ pound shelled cooked shrimp

salt and black pepper

3-4 tbsp chopped fresh mint

shavings of Parmesan cheese

1   Melt the butter in a saucepan, add the shallot and cook until softened. Stir in the curry powder and cook for a further minute.

2   Pour in the wine and boil over a high heat until reduced by half. Stir in the cream and cook gently for about 3 minutes to thicken the sauce.

3   Stir in the shrimp and heat through gently. Season to taste with salt and pepper.

4   Toss the sauce into freshly cooked pasta with the mint. Serve at once, sprinkled with shavings of Parmesan cheese.

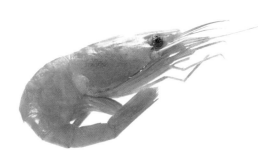

Salmon and Fennel

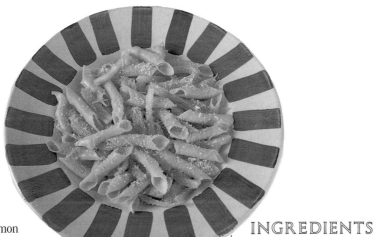

1   Poach the salmon fillet in half the lemon juice and just enough water to cover. To test when cooked, press the point of a knife into the thickest part of the fish - the flesh should just begin to flake. Skin and roughly flake the salmon, then cover and keep warm.

2   Trim the fennel and cut into matchstick strips.

3   Heat the oil in a skillet and fry the fennel for 6-8 minutes. Add the garlic and lemon zest and cook for a further minute. Gently stir the fennel mixture into freshly cooked pasta with the flaked salmon.

4   Season with a little salt, pepper and lemon juice to taste. Garnish with a dusting of Parmesan cheese.

COOK'S TIP
Salmon fillet is readily available in large supermarkets, cut into portions and wrapped.

INGREDIENTS

Serves 3-4

¾ pound salmon fillet

juice of 1 lemon

1 large bulb fennel

6 tbsp olive oil

1 garlic clove, minced

1 tsp finely grated lemon zest

salt and black pepper

freshly grated Parmesan

Tuna and Roasted Tomato

INGREDIENTS

Serves 4

1 pound fresh tuna steaks

3 tbsp olive oil

2 tbsp lemon juice

2 garlic cloves, minced

1 tsp chopped fresh thyme

4 anchovy fillets, drained
and chopped

1 pound small ripe
tomatoes

8-12 ripe olives, pitted
and chopped

½ cup chopped fresh
flat-leaved parsley

1   Cut the tuna into bite-sized pieces. Place in a baking dish.

2   Mix together the oil, lemon juice, garlic, thyme and anchovies. Pour over the tuna and stir well to coat. Leave to marinate for 1 hour.

3   Cook the tuna in its marinade at 400°F for 10-15 minutes until just cooked.

4   Meanwhile, halve the tomatoes. Scoop out and discard the seeds. Place the tomatoes, skin sides up, under a hot broiler and broil until blistered and lightly charred. Slip off the skins and chop the flesh roughly.

5   Toss the tuna and its liquid into freshly cooked pasta with the tomatoes, olives and parsley.

Shrimp with Brandy

1 Melt the butter in a saucepan and cook the shallot until softened. Add the mushrooms and cook briskly for 1-2 minutes. Using a slotted spoon, transfer to a plate and set aside.

2 Pour in the brandy and cook over a high heat until reduced by half. Stir in the cream and bring to a boil, stirring.

3 Reduce the heat, then return the mushrooms and add the shrimp. Heat through gently. Season with salt and pepper.

4 Toss the sauce with freshly cooked pasta and garnish with a sprinkling of chopped fresh parsley.

INGREDIENTS

Serves 4

¼ cup butter

1 shallot, chopped

1 cup button mushrooms

2 tbsp brandy

1¼ cups whipping cream

¾ pound shelled cooked large shrimp

salt and black pepper

fresh chopped parsley to garnish

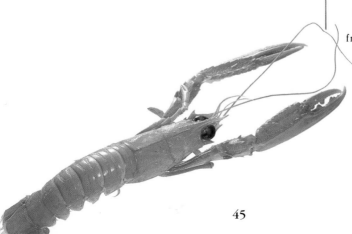

Spiced Shrimp Butter

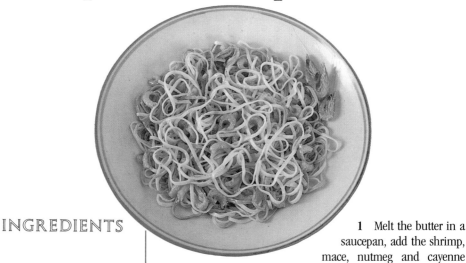

INGREDIENTS

Serves 4 as an appetizer

½ cup sweet butter

2 cups shelled cooked small shrimp

¼ tsp ground mace

¼ tsp freshly grated nutmeg

a generous pinch of cayenne pepper

whole cooked brown shrimp to garnish

1 Melt the butter in a saucepan, add the shrimp, mace, nutmeg and cayenne pepper. Heat gently but do not boil.

2 Toss with freshly cooked pasta. Garnish with whole brown shrimp and serve at once.

COOK'S TIP
If you have shelled the shrimp yourself, make a shellfish butter to add extra flavor to the sauce. Place the shells in a food processor with 2 tbsp of the butter and process to a paste, then press the mixture through a strainer to extract all the butter and juices. Stir into the sauce before tossing with the pasta.

Monkfish with Tarragon

1 Cut the fennel, carrots and zucchini into matchstick strips. Remove the backbone from the monkfish and trim the flesh of all dark skin. Cut into cubes.

2 Heat the oil in a shallow pan. Add the carrots and fennel and fry gently for 3 minutes. Remove the vegetables from the pan and keep warm.

3 Add the monkfish to the pan and fry for 2-3 minutes. Pour in the wine, cover and cook for 4-5 minutes. Remove from the pan and add to the fennel and carrots.

4 Boil the pan juices to reduce by half. Stir in the crème fraîche and cook for 1-2 minutes. Return the vegetables and monkfish to the pan with the zucchini, lemon zest, tarragon and seasoning. Cook for a further 2-3 minutes.

5 Toss the sauce carefully into freshly cooked pasta.

INGREDIENTS

Serves 4

1 small bulb of Florence fennel

2 small carrots

2 small zucchini

1 pound monkfish

¼ cup olive oil

3 tbsp dry white wine

¼ cup crème fraîche

2 tsp finely grated lemon zest

1 tbsp chopped fresh tarragon

salt and black pepper

Mixed Seafood

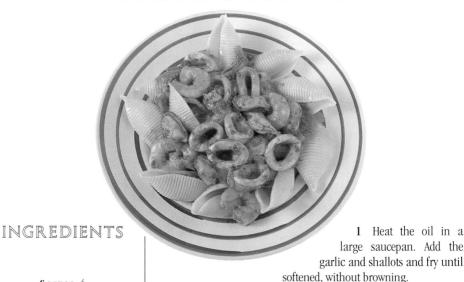

INGREDIENTS

Serves 4

2 tbsp olive oil

2 garlic cloves, minced

2 shallots, chopped

6 tbsp dry white wine

2 cups passata (thick strained tomatoes)

1 bay leaf

2 thyme sprigs

3 dried red chilies

1 pound shellfish, including mussels, shrimp and squid

3 tbsp chopped parsley

pinch of sugar (optional)

1 Heat the oil in a large saucepan. Add the garlic and shallots and fry until softened, without browning.

2 Pour in the wine and tomatoes, then add the bay leaf, thyme and chilies. Bring to a boil, cover and simmer for about 20 minutes, stirring occasionally.

3 Remove and discard the herbs and chilies. Stir in the shellfish and parsley. Return to the heat and warm through gently. Taste and adjust the seasoning, adding salt and black pepper and a pinch of sugar if necessary.

4 Spoon over freshly cooked pasta and serve immediately.

Scallops with Garlic

1 Cut the white flesh of the scallops horizontally into 2 or 3 slices.

2 Heat the oil in a skillet. Add the garlic, leek and red-pepper flakes and fry for 1 minute. Add the scallops and fry for 2-3 minutes; then remove and keep warm.

3 Pour in the wine and cook over a high heat until slightly reduced. Return the scallops to the pan with the parsley and warm through gently. Taste and adjust the seasoning with salt.

4 Toss into freshly cooked pasta and serve at once.

INGREDIENTS

Serves 4 as an appetizer

8-12 shelled scallops

⅓ cup olive oil

3 garlic cloves, minced

1 leek, cut into fine shreds

¼ tsp hot red-pepper flakes

½ cup dry white wine

2 tbsp chopped fresh parsley

salt

Tuna, Bean and Red Onion

INGREDIENTS

Serves 4

¼ cup olive oil

1 red onion, sliced

1 tsp finely grated lemon zest

1 tbsp lemon juice

1 tsp Dijon mustard

14½ oz can cannellini beans, rinsed and drained

7½ oz can tuna in oil, drained and flaked

2 tbsp rinsed and drained capers

4 tbsp chopped parsley

salt and black pepper

grated Parmesan cheese

1 Heat the oil in a skillet and cook the onion until softened, without browning.

2 Stir in the lemon zest and juice, mustard, beans, tuna, capers and parsley. Cook gently until warmed through. Season generously with salt and pepper.

3 Spoon the sauce over freshly cooked pasta and sprinkle with Parmesan cheese.

Anchovy and Golden Crumb

1 Heat the oil in a large skillet. Add the garlic and bread crumbs and stir over a medium heat until golden brown.

2 Stir in the anchovies, olives and parsley.

3 Gently toss the bread crumb mixture into hot pasta and serve.

INGREDIENTS

Serves 4 as an appetizer

2-3 tbsp olive oil

2 garlic cloves, minced

1½ cups fine fresh white bread crumbs

2 oz can anchovy fillets, drained and chopped

12 ripe Greek olives, pitted and sliced

½ cup chopped fresh parsley

Grecian Lamb

INGREDIENTS

Serves 4

2 tbsp olive oil

1 onion, chopped

3 cups cubed lean lamb

2 garlic cloves, minced

1 tsp ground cinnamon

¼ tsp grated nutmeg

1 tbsp tomato paste

6 tbsp dry white wine

1 pound ripe tomatoes

1 bouquet garni

salt, pepper and sugar

1 cup cubed feta cheese

fresh parsley, chopped

1 Heat the oil in a saucepan, add the onion and fry until just beginning to brown. Add the lamb and garlic and cook until evenly browned, stirring occasionally.

2 Stir in the cinnamon, nutmeg, tomato paste, wine, tomatoes, peeled, deseeded and chopped, and the bouquet garni. Bring to a boil, cover and simmer gently, stirring occasionally, for about 30 minutes or until the lamb is tender. Remove the bouquet garni.

3 Taste and adjust the seasoning with a little salt, pepper and sugar. Just before serving scatter the cheese over the top. Serve with freshly cooked pasta and sprinkle with parsley.

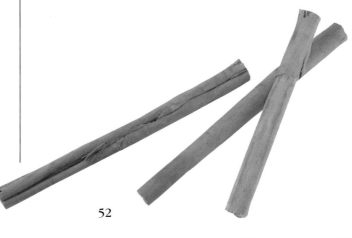

Carbonara

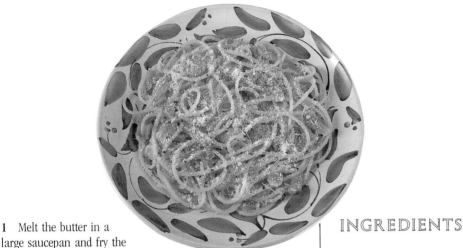

1 Melt the butter in a large saucepan and fry the bacon until lightly colored.

2 Meanwhile, beat together the eggs and half the Parmesan cheese. Season with a little salt.

3 Drain the pasta and return it to the pan. Quickly pour in the egg mixture. Toss well.

4 Add the hot bacon and toss again. Turn the pasta into warmed serving bowls. Grind over some pepper and top with the remaining Parmesan cheese.

COOK'S TIP
The pasta must be very hot when the egg mixture is added so that the eggs cook and thicken slightly.

INGREDIENTS

Serves 4

2 tbsp butter

6 oz lean bacon, cut into strips

4 eggs

salt and black pepper

3/4 cup freshly grated Parmesan cheese

Proscuitto and Sage

INGREDIENTS

Serves 2

2 tbsp butter

1 tbsp olive oil

2 garlic cloves, chopped

3oz proscuitto, cut into strips

1 tbsp chopped fresh sage

black pepper

2 tbsp freshly grated Parmesan cheese

1 Heat the butter and oil in a skillet. Add the garlic, proscuitto and sage and fry for 2-3 minutes. Season with plenty of freshly ground black pepper.

2 Toss into freshly cooked pasta with the Parmesan cheese and serve at once.

COOK'S TIP
If proscuitto (Italian dry, cured ham) is unavailable, try using lean, cooked ham.

Chicken Livers with Marsala

1 Heat the butter and oil in a skillet and fry the shallot until softened. Add the bacon and continue frying for a further 2 minutes, turning occasionally.

2 Add the chicken livers and fry for 1-2 minutes until they are evenly browned.

3 Pour in the Marsala and add the sage and capers. Allow to bubble for a few minutes. Taste and adjust the seasoning with salt and pepper.

4 Serve with freshly cooked pasta and garnish with chopped, flat-leaved parsley.

COOK'S TIP
Do not overcook the chicken livers; they should still be pink in the center.

INGREDIENTS

Serves 2-3

2 tbsp butter

2 tbsp olive oil

1 shallot, chopped

2 slices bacon, chopped

$1/2$ pound chicken livers, trimmed and chopped

$1/4$ cup Marsala

2 tsp chopped fresh sage

2 tbsp drained and rinsed capers

salt and black pepper

fresh flat-leaved parsley, chopped

Hot Bacon

INGREDIENTS

Serves 4

2 tbsp olive oil

½ pound bacon, chopped

2 garlic cloves, crushed

2 fresh red chilies, deseeded and chopped

1½ pounds ripe tomatoes, peeled, deseeded and chopped

2 tbsp tomato paste

salt and black pepper

2 tbsp fresh mixed herbs (basil, parsley and marjoram), chopped

1 Heat the oil in a saucepan and fry the bacon until golden brown. Add the garlic and chilies and cook for a further 2 minutes stirring occasionally.

2 Stir in the tomatoes, tomato paste and seasoning. Cook, uncovered, for about 15 minutes until the sauce has thickened.

3 Toss the bacon sauce into freshly cooked pasta with the herbs. Serve at once.

COOK'S TIP
When preparing chilies, it's a good idea to wear rubber gloves because the juice can irritate the skin. Do not let a chili get anywhere near the eyes, even via your fingers.

Chicken and Herb Cream

1 Gently heat the crème fraîche in a small saucepan until just beginning to boil. Remove from the heat and stir in the parsley, basil and tarragon. Leave to infuse while cooking the chicken.

2 Heat the oil and butter in a skillet. Add the chicken strips and stir-fry over a high heat for 4-5 minutes until cooked through. Add the garlic and cook, stirring for a further minute.

3 Stir in the herb cream and warm through. Season with salt and pepper to taste.

4 Toss into freshly cooked pasta and serve sprinkled with Parmesan cheese.

INGREDIENTS

Serves 4

1¼ cups crème fraîche or sour cream

3 tbsp chopped fresh parsley

3 tbsp shredded fresh basil

1½ tbsp chopped fresh tarragon

1 tbsp olive oil

2 tbsp butter

1 pound chicken breast fillets, cut into strips

2 garlic cloves, minced

salt and black pepper

freshly grated Parmesan cheese

Salami, Feta and Olives

INGREDIENTS

Serves 4

¼ cup olive oil

2 tbsp pesto (see page 22)

12 slices Italian salami, cut into strips

½ cup garlic-flavored ripe olives, pitted and roughly chopped

1 cup cubed feta cheese

black pepper

flat-leaved parsley sprigs

1   Heat the oil with the pesto in a small saucepan until bubbling.

2   Toss into freshly cooked pasta with the salami, olives and feta.

3   Grind over some black pepper and serve at once, garnished with flat-leaved parsley sprigs.

COOK'S TIP
Use store-bought pesto sauce for a really speedy recipe.

Confit of Duck and Mushroom

1   Lift out the pieces of confit from its container and remove as much fat as possible. Cut away the flesh in neat pieces.

2   Heat the duck fat in a skillet, add the garlic and mushrooms and fry for 2-3 minutes. Stir in the duck pieces and heat through.

3   Toss into freshly cooked pasta with the parsley. Grind some pepper over and serve with a sprinkling of Parmesan cheese.

Serves 2

2-3 pieces confit of duck

¼ cup fat from the confit

2 garlic cloves, minced

1½ cups mixed mushrooms, such as brown cap and oyster, sliced

1 tbsp chopped fresh parsley

black pepper

freshly grated Parmesan cheese

Veal and Jerusalem Artichoke

INGREDIENTS

Serves 4

¾ pound veal scaloppini,
trimmed

2 tbsp olive oil

2oz proscuitto, cut into
strips

1 shallot, chopped

1 cup peeled and thinly
sliced Jerusalem
artichokes

1 zucchini, diced

1 cup whipping cream

1 tbsp shredded fresh
basil

salt and black pepper

½ cup pine nuts, toasted

1   Lay the veal between sheets of dampened waxed paper and beat gently until thin. Cut into thin slices using a very sharp knife.

2   Heat the oil in a large skillet. Add the veal slices and proscuitto and stir-fry for 2-3 minutes only. Remove from the pan with a slotted spoon and keep warm.

3   Add the shallot and Jerusalem artichokes and stir-fry for 3-4 minutes. Add the zucchini and cook for a further 2 minutes until the vegetables are tender but still crisp.

4   Pour in the cream and add the basil. Return the veal and proscuitto to the pan and heat through gently. Taste and adjust the seasoning, adding a little salt, if necessary, and black pepper to taste.

5   Spoon over freshly cooked pasta. Sprinkle with the toasted pine nuts and serve at once.

COOK'S TIP
To prepare Jerusalem artichokes, scrub them well, then peel thinly. As you peel them drop them into a bowl of water acidulated with a little lemon juice to prevent discoloration.

Bolognese

1 Heat the oil in a saucepan, add the onion, carrot and garlic and fry until soft but not browned.

2 Add bacon, chopped chicken livers and ground beef and cook until the meat loses its raw color.

3 Pour in the wine and cook gently until it has evaporated. Add the milk and cook until absorbed into the sauce. Stir in the tomatoes, tomato paste, bouquet garni and seasoning. Cover and cook over a very low heat for about 1 hour, stirring occasionally. Add water if necessary so the sauce is not dry. Discard the bouquet garni and adjust the seasoning.

4 Spoon the sauce over freshly cooked pasta and serve with Parmesan cheese sprinkled on top.

INGREDIENTS

Serves 4

3 tbsp olive oil

1 onion, chopped

1 carrot, finely chopped

2 garlic cloves, minced

2 oz unsmoked bacon, chopped

2 oz chicken livers

3/4 pound ground beef

1 1/4 cups dry white wine

1/2 cup milk

1 pound ripe tomatoes

1 tbsp tomato paste

1 bouquet garni

Beef with Basil

INGREDIENTS

Serves 4

3 tbsp oyster sauce

1 tbsp dark soy sauce

½ cup beef broth

1 garlic clove, minced

1 pound rump steak, cut into bite-sized pieces

1½ cups halved snap beans

3 tbsp peanut oil

2 tbsp shredded fresh basil

1 tsp cornstarch

1 tbsp sesame oil

Szechwan peppercorns, roasted and ground

1 Mix together the oyster sauce, soy sauce, beef broth and garlic in a shallow dish. Add the beef and toss well. Leave to marinate for about 30 minutes.

2 Blanch the beans in boiling salted water for 1 minute, then refresh under cold water. Drain well.

3 Heat the peanut oil in a wok or skillet and cook the beef mixture for 2-3 minutes. Add the beans and basil and stir-fry for 2 minutes.

4 Mix the cornstarch with 1 tbsp water and stir into the sauce. Cook a further minute until thickened. Stir in the sesame oil and Szechwan peppercorns to taste.

5 Serve immediately with freshly cooked pasta.

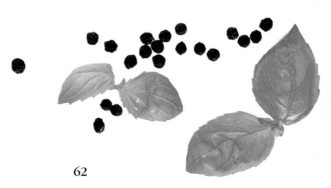

Ham, Spinach and Ricotta

1 Melt half the butter in a skillet and fry the garlic until just beginning to color but not brown.

2 Add the smoked ham and spinach and fry for 1-2 minutes.

3 Melt the remaining butter in a separate saucepan, add the ricotta and cook, stirring, until heated through.

4 Tip the freshly cooked pasta into the ricotta and toss thoroughly. Stir in the smoked ham and spinach mixture. Season with nutmeg, a little salt if needed and pepper to taste.

5 Serve at once, sprinkled with shavings of Parmesan cheese.

COOK'S TIP
Be careful not to overcook the spinach, as it quickly loses its characteristic texture and flavor.

INGREDIENTS

Serves 4

½ cup butter

1 garlic clove, minced

8 oz wafer-thin smoked ham, cut into strips

4½ cups roughly chopped young spinach leaves

¾ cup ricotta cheese

freshly grated nutmeg

salt and black pepper

shavings of Parmesan cheese

Spicy Sausage and Tomato

INGREDIENTS

Serves 4

2 tbsp olive oil

1 pound spicy fresh
Italian sausages, thickly
sliced

1 onion, chopped

2 garlic cloves, minced

1 red bell pepper,
deseeded and cubed

1½ pounds ripe tomatoes,
peeled, deseeded and
chopped

2 tbsp tomato paste

1 tbsp chopped fresh
oregano

shavings of Parmesan
cheese (optional)
oregano sprigs

1 Heat the oil in a large saucepan, add the sausage slices and cook until beginning to brown.

2 Add the onion, garlic and pepper; cook, stirring, until softened. Stir in the tomatoes, tomato paste, oregano and seasoning of salt and black pepper. Bring to a boil, cover and cook for 15-20 minutes.

3 Spoon the sauce onto freshly cooked pasta and serve with shavings of Parmesan cheese. Garnish with oregano sprigs.

Pork Paprika

1 Place the peppers under a hot broiler for 10 minutes, turning occasionally, until evenly blistered and charred. Cool slightly, then peel away and discard skins. Cut peppers in half, discard the seeds and cut the flesh into squares. Set aside.

2 Heat the oil and butter in a large skillet, add the onion and pork and fry until the pork is evenly browned.

3 Add the garlic and paprika and cook for a further minute. Stir in the tomato paste and stock. Cook for about 10 minutes until the pork is tender.

4 Stir in the peppers and seasoning to taste. Heat through gently until piping hot.

5 Serve at once with freshly cooked pasta, topping each portion with a spoonful of sour cream or crème fraîche if liked. Garnish with chopped parsley.

COOK'S TIP
Replace the pork with 1 pound chicken breast meat, sliced.

INGREDIENTS

Serves 4

2 large red bell peppers

2 tbsp olive oil

1 onion, chopped

1 pound pork tenderloin, trimmed and thinly sliced

1 garlic clove, minced

1 tbsp paprika

2 tsp tomato paste

$2/3$ cup bouillon

salt and black pepper

$1/2$ cup sour cream or crème fraîche (optional)

chopped fresh parsley

Hunter's Chicken

INGREDIENTS

Serves 4

2 tbsp olive oil

1 onion, chopped

2 garlic cloves, minced

1 pound chicken breast meat, sliced

1¼ cups passata (thick strained tomatoes)

6 tbsp dry white wine

2 oz prosciutto, cut into strips (optional)

2 tsp fresh rosemary

1 tsp chopped fresh thyme

2 cups flat mushrooms

rosemary sprigs

1 Heat the oil in a saucepan and fry the onion until softened. Add the garlic and chicken and cook for 2-3 minutes.

2 Pour in the tomatoes and wine, then add the prosciutto, if using, chopped rosemary, thyme and seasoning of salt and black pepper. Bring to a boil, then cover and simmer for 8 minutes.

3 Add the mushrooms and cook for a further 2 minutes. Spoon onto freshly cooked pasta and sprinkle with Parmesan cheese. Garnish with rosemary sprigs and serve at once.

Sausage and Cream

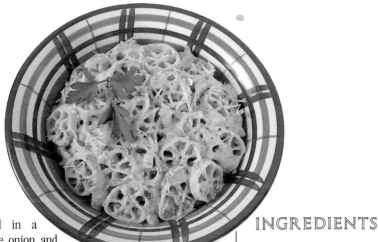

1 Heat the oil in a saucepan, add the onion and fry gently until soft but not browned.

2 Remove the skins from the sausages and add the meat to the pan with the wine. Cook gently for 10-12 minutes, breaking up the sausages with a fork.

3 Stir in the cream and parsley and simmer until the sauce thickens. Remove the pan from the heat and leave for 5 minutes to allow the flavors to infuse. Taste and adjust the seasoning.

4 Toss the sauce with freshly cooked pasta and sprinkle with the Parmesan cheese. Garnish with flat-leaved parsley sprigs.

INGREDIENTS

Serves 4

1 tbsp olive oil

1 onion, chopped

½ pound good-quality pork sausages

½ cup dry white wine

1¼ cups whipping cream

2 tbsp fresh parsley, (preferably flat-leaved), chopped

salt and black pepper

⅓ cup freshly grated Parmesan cheese

flat-leaved parsley sprigs to garnish

Pork with Mustard and Pepper

INGREDIENTS

Serves 4

3 tbsp olive oil

1 pound pork tenderloin,
trimmed and thinly sliced

1/4 cup butter

1 garlic clove, minced

2 shallots, chopped

2 cups sliced button
mushrooms

2 tsp green peppercorns
in brine, rinsed and
lightly crushed

2 tbsp wholegrain mustard

1/4 cup whipping cream

salt

snipped fresh chives

1   Heat the oil in a large skillet. Add the pork in batches and brown evenly. Remove from the pan using a slotted spoon which drains away the oil.

2   Add the butter then the garlic and shallots and cook until softened. Stir in the mushrooms, peppercorns and mustard and gently fry for 2 minutes.

3   Return the pork to the pan and stir in the cream. Heat through until piping hot. Taste and adjust the seasoning.

4   Serve with freshly cooked pasta, garnished with chives.

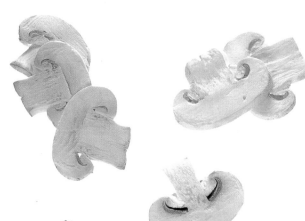

Walnut

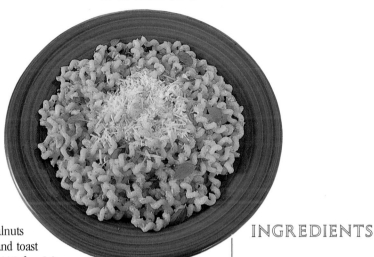

1 Spread the walnuts on a baking tray and toast in the oven at 350°F for 5-8 minutes. Cool slightly.

2 Put the walnuts, butter and garlic in a blender or food processor and process to form a coarse paste.

3 With the machine still running, gradually add the oil. Transfer the walnut mixture to a bowl and stir in the cream, Parmesan cheese and oregano. Season with salt and black pepper.

4 Spoon the sauce over freshly cooked pasta and toss well. Serve with extra Parmesan cheese and garnish with oregano sprigs.

INGREDIENTS

Serves 4

1 cup shelled walnuts, roughly chopped

6 tbsp butter, softened

1 garlic clove, roughly chopped

3 tbsp olive oil

3 tbsp whipping cream

$1/2$ cup freshly grated Parmesan cheese

$1/2$ tsp chopped fresh oregano

salt and black pepper

freshly grated Parmesan cheese to serve

oregano sprigs

Ricotta and Walnut

INGREDIENTS

Serves 4

¼ cup butter

¾ cup walnuts, roughly chopped

1 ½ cups ricotta cheese

black pepper

freshly grated Parmesan cheese (optional)

1   Melt half the butter in a small skillet and sauté the walnuts until golden brown, turning occasionally.

2   Melt the remaining butter in a large saucepan, add the cheese and cook, stirring, until heated through and smooth. Do not boil. Add the freshly cooked pasta and toss well.

3   Transfer to warmed serving plates, scatter the hot nuts over and grind plenty of pepper over. Serve at once with freshly grated Parmesan cheese, if liked.

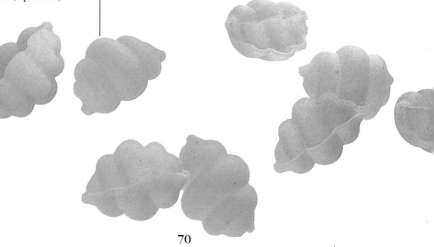

Gorgonzola and Sage

1 Melt the butter in a saucepan, add the garlic and cook on a low heat for 1 minute without browning.

2 Add two-thirds of the cheese, then the cream and sage. Cook, stirring, until the cheese has melted.

3 Season with a little salt, if necessary, pepper and nutmeg.

4 Spoon the sauce over freshly cooked pasta. Sprinkle over the remaining cheese and serve at once.

INGREDIENTS

Serves 4

2 tbsp butter

1 garlic clove, minced

6 oz gorgonzola cheese, derinded and roughly chopped

1¼ cups light cream

2 tsp chopped fresh sage

salt and black pepper

freshly grated nutmeg

Goat Cheese and Prosciutto

Serves 4

¹/₂ pound goat cheese,
sliced

3 tbsp olive oil

2 garlic cloves, minced

2 oz prosciutto, cut into
strips

3 oz sun-dried tomatoes
in oil (drained weight),
chopped

1 tbsp shredded fresh
basil

black pepper

basil sprigs to garnish

1   Line a broiler with foil, then arrange the cheese slices on top. Broil for 3-4 minutes until golden brown and sizzling. Reserve for Step 3.

2   Meanwhile, heat the oil, add the garlic and fry for a few minutes. Add the ham and sun-dried tomatoes and fry until the ham begins to frizzle.

3   Add the ham and tomato mixture to freshly cooked pasta with the basil. Transfer to warmed serving plates and top each with a slice of cheese.

4   Grind some pepper over. Garnish with basil sprigs and serve.

COOK'S TIP
Choose a goat cheese with a rind for this recipe, because it will help the cheese keep its shape when it is broiled.

Butter and Cheese

1 Melt the butter in
a saucepan. Add the
freshly cooked pasta and toss
gently over a low heat until evenly
coated with butter sauce.

2 Transfer to warmed serving plates and sprinkle the grated
Parmesan cheese over. Toss gently and serve at once, garnished
with sage leaves.

INGREDIENTS

Serves 3-4

½ cup butter

1 cup freshly grated
Parmesan cheese

fresh sage leaves
to garnish

Four Cheeses

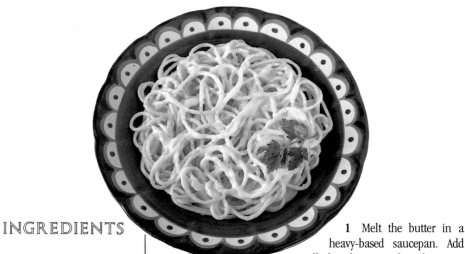

INGREDIENTS

Serves 4

2 tbsp butter

⅓ cup grated Parmesan
cheese

¼ cup derinded and diced
dolcelatte cheese

¼ cup grated mozzarella
cheese

⅓ cup grated Gruyère
cheese

⅔ cup whipping cream

black pepper

flat-leaved parsley sprigs
to garnish

1 Melt the butter in a heavy-based saucepan. Add all the cheeses and cook over a very low heat, stirring until melted. Don't worry if the mixture separates; this will not affect the finished dish.

2 Gradually pour in the cream, beating well until it forms a smooth sauce. Slowly bring to a boil, then cook on a lower heat until the sauce thickens.

3 Pour the sauce over freshly cooked pasta and toss together until the strands of pasta are evenly coated. Serve at once, garnished with parsley sprigs.

Goat Cheese with Watercress

1 Beat together the goat cheese and cream until smooth. Melt the butter in a large saucepan, add the cheese mixture and cook, stirring, until warmed through.

2 Drain the hot pasta and toss in the cheese mixture until the pasta is evenly coated.

3 Add the watercress and toss again. Grind over pepper to taste and serve at once.

INGREDIENTS

Serves 4

5oz mild French goat cheese

⅔ cup light cream

2 tbsp butter

¾ cup roughly chopped watercress

black pepper

Parmesan Cream

INGREDIENTS

Serves 4

3 tbsp butter

1/4 cup all-purpose flour

1 1/4 cups milk

1/2 cup freshly grated
Parmesan cheese

2 egg yolks

2/3 cup whipping cream

salt and white pepper

freshly grated Parmesan
cheese to serve

1   Melt the butter in a saucepan. Stir in the flour and cook gently for a few minutes.

2   Gradually add the milk, bring to a boil and simmer for a few minutes. Remove from the heat and stir in the cheese.

3   Mix the egg yolks with the cream and stir into the sauce. Reheat very gently, stirring continuously. Do not boil. Taste and adjust the seasoning.

4   Spoon the sauce over freshly cooked pasta. Sprinkle with grated Parmesan cheese and serve at once.

Dolcelatte and Pine Nut

1 Spread the pine nuts on a baking tray and toast for 3-5 minutes, turning occasionally, until golden brown. Set aside.

2 Melt the butter in a heavy-based saucepan. Add the cheese and cook, stirring, over a low heat until melted.

3 Gradually add the cream, stirring to form a smooth sauce. Season with pepper to taste.

4 Toss the sauce into freshly cooked pasta with the chives. Sprinkle the toasted pine nuts over the top and serve at once.

COOK'S TIP
If Torta di Dolcelatte is unavailable use Dolcelatte or Gorgonzola cheese, cut into small cubes so that it melts easily to produce a smooth creamy sauce.

INGREDIENTS

Serves 4

½ cup pine nuts

2 tbsp butter

6 oz Torta di Dolcelatte

½ cup whipping cream

black pepper

2 tbsp snipped fresh chives

Mascarpone and Herb

INGREDIENTS

Serves 4

2 tbsp butter

1 cup Mascarpone cheese

1 cup chopped fresh
mixed herbs, such as
parsley, basil, tarragon
and chives

¼ cup shelled pistachio
nuts, finely chopped

¼ cup grated Parmesan
cheese

salt and black pepper

1   Melt the butter in a pan, add the Mascarpone cheese and cook, stirring, until warmed through.

2   Pour the cheese mixture over freshly cooked pasta and toss.

3   Sprinkle over most of the herbs, leaving some for the garnish, the pistachio nuts and Parmesan cheese. Toss well. Taste and adjust the seasoning with salt and pepper.

4   Serve at once with the remaining herbs sprinkled over.

Alfredo

1 Melt the butter in a small saucepan. Add the cream and bring almost to a boil stirring occasionally.

2 Drain the pasta and return it to the pan. Pour in the butter and cream mixture and toss until the pasta is evenly coated.

3 Add the Parmesan cheese, a pinch of grated nutmeg and plenty of pepper. Toss again to mix. Serve at once with grated Parmesan cheese sprinkled on top.

INGREDIENTS

Serves 4

¼ cup butter

1 cup whipping cream

1 ½ cup freshly grated
Parmesan cheese

freshly grated nutmeg

black pepper

freshly grated
Parmesan
cheese

79

Index

Alfredo 79
Anchovy and Golden
  Crumb 51
Asparagus with Proscuitto
  17

Beef with Basil 62
Bolognese 61
Borlotti Bean and
  Mushroom 19
Butter and Cheese 73

Carbonara 53
Chicken and Herb Cream 57
Chicken Livers with
  Marsala 55
Chick-pea with Coriander 31
Chili-Shrimp with Snow
  Peas 36
Chili-Tomato with Olives 23
Confit of Duck and
  Mushroom 59
Crab with Chive 38
Creamy Broccoli 30

Dolcelatte and Pine Nut 77

Four Cheeses 74

Garlic and Oil 21
Goat Cheese and Proscuitto
  72
Goat Cheese with
  Watercress 75
Golden Onion with

Rosemary 24
Gorgonzola and Sage 71
Grecian Lamb 52

Ham, Spinach and
  Ricotta 63
Hot Bacon 56
Hunter's Chicken 66

Leek and Pancetta 18

Marinated Tomato and
  Herb 10
Mascarpone and Herb 78
Mediterranean Squid 41
Mixed Mushroom 28
Mixed Seafood 48
Monkfish with Tarragon 47

Parmesan Cream 76
Pea and Ham 33
Pepper and Mozzarella 12
Peppers with Saffron and
  Basil 20
Pesto 22
Pink Shrimp 34
Pork Paprika 65
Pork with Mustard and
  Pepper 68
Proscuitto and Sage 54

Red Clam 37
Ricotta and Walnut 70
Roasted Fennel with
  Lemon 11

Roasted Garlic and Herb 13

Saffron-Mussel 40
Salami, Feta and Olives 58
Salmon and Fennel 43
Sausage and Cream 67
Scallop with Garlic 49
Shredded Zucchini 29
Shrimp with Brandy 45
Shrimp in Curried
  Cream 42
Sicilian Cauliflower 15
Smoked Salmon and Dill 39
Smoked Trout with
  Avocado 35
Spiced Shrimp Butter 46
Spicy Avocado 32
Spicy Sausage and
  Tomato 64
Spring Vegetable 14
Sun-dried Tomato and
  Shallot 16

Tapenade 26
Tofu with Cashew Nut 27
Tomato and Basil 25
Tuna and Roasted
  Tomato 44
Tuna, Bean and Red
  Onion 50

Veal and Jerusalem
  Artichoke 60

Walnut 69